NFL
TODAY

THE STORY OF THE
CINCINNATI BENGALS

NFL TODAY

THE STORY OF THE CINCINNATI BENGALS

SARA GILBERT

CREATIVE EDUCATION

Cover: Wide receiver Chad Johnson (top),
quarterback Carson Palmer (bottom)
Page 2: Wide receiver Antonio Chatman
Pages 4–5: Bengals offense, 1969
Pages 6–7: Bengals defense, 2008

....

Published by Creative Education
P.O. Box 227, Mankato, Minnesota 56002
Creative Education is an imprint of
The Creative Company
www.thecreativecompany.us

Design and production by Blue Design
Design Associate: Sarah Yakawonis
Printed in the United States of America

Photographs by Getty Images (Sylvia Allen/
NFL, Al Bello, Scott Boehm, Clifton Boutelle/NFL
Photos, Peter Brouillet/NFL, Kevin C. Cox, Diamond
Images, Ned Dishman, David Drapkin, Elsa, George
Gojkovich, Otto Greule Jr./Allsport, Scott Halleran/
Allsport, Tom Hauck, Andy Lyons, Al Messerschmidt,
Al Messerschmidt/NFL, Donald Miralle, NFL, Peter
Pearson, Joe Robbins, George Rose, Manny Rubio/
NFL, Dilip Vishwanat)

Library of Congress Cataloging-in-Publication Data

Gilbert, Sara.
The story of the Cincinnati Bengals / by Sara
Gilbert.
p. cm. — (NFL today)
Includes index.
ISBN 978-1-58341-751-5
1. Cincinnati Bengals (Football team)—History—
Juvenile literature. I. Title. II. Series.

GV956.C6G554 2008
796.332'640977178—dc22   2008022682

First Edition
9 8 7 6 5 4 3 2 1

CONTENTS

ON THE SIDELINES

MEET THE BENGALS

BEGINNING WITH BROWN

When Cincinnati, Ohio, was first founded on the Ohio River in 1788, it was one of the first major cities to thrive in America's heartland. Because the United States did not yet stretch from coast to coast, Cincinnati became known as "The Queen City of the West." As the country's geographic boundaries moved westward, however, that nickname was shortened to simply "Queen City."

Among the many jewels in the city's crown are its professional sports teams. In 1869, the city became home to the country's first pro baseball team, the Cincinnati Reds. In the early 1900s, Cincinnati was also home to three different pro football teams, including a club known as the Bengals. That team folded in 1942, but when a new professional franchise was established as part of the American Football League (AFL) in Cincinnati in 1968, it was promptly given the name of its predecessor: the Cincinnati Bengals.

The Bengals team that first took the field in September 1968 was a combination of veteran players who were

X Cincinnati, a town that has gone by various nicknames (it was called "Porkopolis" in the mid-1800s due to its busy pork-packing business), has long been known as a great sports city.

obtained in an expansion draft—such as cornerback Charlie King and offensive guard Pat Matson—and young rookies, including running back Paul Robinson, who scored Cincinnati's first touchdown on a two-yard rush against the San Diego Chargers in the season opener. Leading them all was Paul Brown, the Bengals' owner, general manager, and coach, who had already tallied a 158–48–8 career record and three National Football League (NFL) championships with the Cleveland Browns. His hope was to find similar success in Cincinnati.

Although Robinson led the AFL with 1,023 rushing yards and was honored as the Rookie of the Year, the 1968 Bengals finished with a disappointing 3–11 record. But with the addition of linebacker Bill Bergey and quarterback Greg Cook in the 1969 NFL Draft, the Bengals (who, along with the rest of the AFL, had merged with the NFL) quickly improved to an 8–6 record in 1970, earning the American Football Conference (AFC) Central Division title and making their first trip to the playoffs. With Cook sidelined by a shoulder injury that would soon end his career, the Bengals lost 17–0 to the eventual Super Bowl champion Baltimore Colts.

The success of that season was duplicated two years later, this time with young quarterback Ken Anderson under center. Thanks to Anderson's pinpoint accuracy, the speed of

PAUL BROWN

COACH
BENGALS SEASONS: 1968-75

Paul Brown had already done everything a football coach could want to do. His teams had dominated at every level of the game, from high school to college to professional. He had won four All-America Football Conference and three NFL title games as coach of the Cleveland Browns. But in 1967, the same year that he was elected to the Pro Football Hall of Fame, Brown decided to do more. Four years after he was fired as head coach of the Browns, he returned to football as the principal owner, general manager, and coach of the Cincinnati Bengals, which at the time was part of the AFL. Success wasn't as immediate for Brown with the Bengals, who joined the NFL in 1970. He stepped down as head coach in 1976 but stayed on as team president, witnessing Cincinnati's two trips to the Super Bowl in the 1980s. Brown remained with the Bengals until his death in 1991 of complications from pneumonia. His son Mike then took over the team.

THE ORIGINAL BENGALS

When Paul Brown brought professional football back to Cincinnati in 1968 after a 26-year absence, he gave the new team a familiar name. The original Cincinnati Bengals played in an earlier American Football League from 1937 until 1942. Those Bengals were actually the third professional football team to call Cincinnati home. First came the Celts in 1921, followed by the Reds in 1933 and 1934. The first Bengals team lasted longer and drew larger crowds than its predecessors but played in a financially troubled league that went bankrupt after the 1937 season. The AFL reinvented itself in 1939 (and again in 1940), but by 1942, as the United States was preparing to enter World War II, the league and the Bengals were done for good. When Brown announced the formation of a new Cincinnati franchise, fans suggested hundreds of possibilities for its name—including Buckeyes, the name of Ohio State University's team. Brown, however, already had a name in mind. It would be Bengals, he said, "to give it a link with past professional football in Cincinnati."

halfback Essex Johnson, and the sure hands of rookie receiver Isaac Curtis, the 1973 Bengals won 10 games and made it to the playoffs again. This time, it was the Miami Dolphins who eliminated Cincinnati in the first round.

Anderson developed into one of the finest passers in football, finding favorite targets such as Curtis and tight end Bob Trumpy so frequently that he earned the first of his four trips to the Pro Bowl during the 1975 season. Led by Anderson, the team put together an impressive 11–3 record that year and made its third appearance in the playoffs. But once again, the Bengals were beaten in the first round, a

X As a rookie in 1968, Paul Robinson became just the second football player ever to rush for more than 1,000 yards in his first pro season—an achievement that made him an AFL All-Star.

X Big running back Pete Johnson (left) was a football hero in Ohio for 11 years—he spent 4 seasons as a college star at Ohio State University and 7 seasons in a Bengals uniform.

close 31–28 loss to the Oakland Raiders on December 28. Four days later, on New Year's Day, Coach Brown surprised players and fans alike when he announced that he was stepping down as coach so that he could concentrate on being general manager. He turned his on-field duties over to Bill Johnson, who had been an assistant coach since the team's beginning.

Anderson remained one of the best quarterbacks in the league, and bruising fullback Pete Johnson strengthened the Bengals' running game, but Cincinnati wasn't good enough to get back to the playoffs until 1981. Then, as they introduced their new tiger-striped uniforms, the Bengals roared back into contention with a 12–4 record. Linebacker Reggie Williams led a stingy defense, receiver Cris Collinsworth brought energy to the offense, and Anderson set new team records for passing yards (3,754) and touchdown passes (29) in a season. The Bengals won their division and returned to the playoffs.

KEN ANDERSON

QUARTERBACK
BENGALS SEASONS: 1971-86
HEIGHT: 6-FOOT-2
WEIGHT: 212 POUNDS

Ken Anderson played in one Super Bowl and four Pro Bowls, but it may be his performance in a 1975 Monday Night Football game that Cincinnati fans remember best. Anderson, who earned the starting job in 1972, steadily improved under the instruction of renowned quarterbacks coach Bill Walsh. When the team took the field that Monday night in 1975, Anderson threw for a franchise-record 447 yards in the Bengals' 33–24 win over the Buffalo Bills. In 1981, Anderson started the season with three interceptions in the first half of the first game—and almost lost his starting position to the third-string quarterback. But he rebounded to throw for 3,754 total yards and 29 touchdowns as he led the Bengals to the Super Bowl that season. "You judge people by how they get up after getting knocked down," said former Bengals offensive lineman Dave Lapham, "and he got up and was league MVP [Most Valuable Player]." Anderson retired as a player in 1986 but returned to Cincinnati as a coach from 1993 through 2002. As of 2008, he was the quarterbacks coach for the Pittsburgh Steelers.

✗ Although the Bengals came up short on the scoreboard, Ken Anderson played well in Super Bowl XVI, completing 25 passes (a Super Bowl record at the time) for 300 yards.

This time, Cincinnati refused to lose in the first round. The Bengals, led by head coach Forrest Gregg, toppled the Buffalo Bills 28–21 to advance to the AFC Championship Game. Hosting the San Diego Chargers in subzero temperatures at Cincinnati's Riverfront Stadium, the Bengals won in a lopsided 27–7 tilt. Suddenly, the Bengals were bound for the Super Bowl.

At halftime of Super Bowl XVI in January 1982, the Bengals trailed the San Francisco 49ers 20–0. In an amazing second-half comeback, Cincinnati scored 21 points. But a pair of San Francisco field goals put the game out of reach; when the clock expired, Cincinnati had lost 26–21. After the game, Coach Gregg reassured his disappointed players. "You guys played one heck of a second half," he told them. "Everybody in Cincinnati is proud of you, and you should take pride in yourselves."

Although a players' strike shortened the 1982 season, the Bengals' 7–2 record was good enough to send them to the playoffs again, where the New York Jets quickly eliminated them. Then the offense sputtered, and the 1983 season started with six losses in the first seven weeks. Gregg resigned at the end of the season, and Bengals fans prepared for a changing of the guard in Cincinnati.

THE
ESIASON ERA

X-------------------------------------

X Sam Wyche found more success as an NFL coach than he had as a player; directing such stars as Boomer Esiason (right), Wyche won a team-record 64 games in Cincinnati.

Sam Wyche, who had been a backup quarterback on the Bengals' roster from 1968 to 1970, started his coaching career just as Anderson was ending his playing days. Wyche's first job was to groom the successor for Cincinnati's beloved quarterback, a rookie named Boomer Esiason, who had been picked in the second round of the 1984 NFL Draft.

Esiason had a cannon for an arm and a healthy dose of confidence to match. After injuries sidelined both Anderson and backup Turk Schonert midway through the 1984 season, Esiason eagerly accepted the opportunity to start. "I don't expect to throw five touchdown passes," he told reporters before his first game, "but I also don't expect to throw five interceptions."

Esiason took over as the full-time starting quarterback in 1985 and quickly made an impression. He threw for 3,443 yards and 27 touchdowns that season—but he had help. Esiason was protected by an offensive line anchored by Anthony Muñoz, a mountain of a man who was quick, strong, and smart. And balancing Esiason's aerial strikes were the

[19]

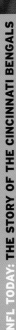

ON THE SIDELINES

BENGALS VERSUS BROWNS

It was only natural that a rivalry would spring up between the Cincinnati Bengals and the Cleveland Browns. For one, both teams are based in Ohio and are not even 250 miles apart. Both teams' players wear the same shade of orange on their uniforms. Both teams have ties to Paul Brown, who was the first coach for both. And because they play in the same division—the AFC North—they play each other regularly enough to keep the rivalry going. Although the all-time series between the Bengals and the Browns was even at 34 wins apiece by 2008, the balance has swung over the years as each team has gone through good and bad periods. Cincinnati wide receiver Cris Collinsworth remembered how important beating the Browns was in 1981, when the Bengals clinched a division title with a 41–21 win at Cleveland Municipal Stadium. "For Paul Brown, that was something special," Collinsworth said. "Every time we went back to Cleveland, he would have never said it publicly, but you knew it meant a little something more to him."

ground attacks of James Brooks, who rushed for more than 1,000 yards in 1986. The Bengals' 10–6 record that year was an improvement, but it wasn't good enough to take the team back to the playoffs.

Another strike in 1987 slowed the momentum that had been building in Cincinnati. After the season resumed in October, the Bengals cobbled together a 4–11 record, highlighted only by the success of kicker Jim Breech, whose 97 points scored was tops in the league, and the announcement that both Muñoz and nose tackle Tim Krumrie had been named to the Pro Bowl. Although it was the first such honor for Krumrie, it was the seventh straight selection for Muñoz, who would be sent to the Pro Bowl 11 times in his 13-year career.

Muñoz was a key part of the turnaround that resulted in the Bengals' remarkable 12–4 record in 1988. So was a re-energized Esiason, who connected with receivers such as Eddie Brown and Tim McGee for a total of 3,572 passing yards and 28 touchdowns. Perhaps more important than either veteran, however, was rookie running back Elbert "Ickey" Woods, whose hustle during training camp had earned him a spot in the starting lineup. Woods led the team with 1,066 rushing yards and scored 15 touchdowns. After each one, he

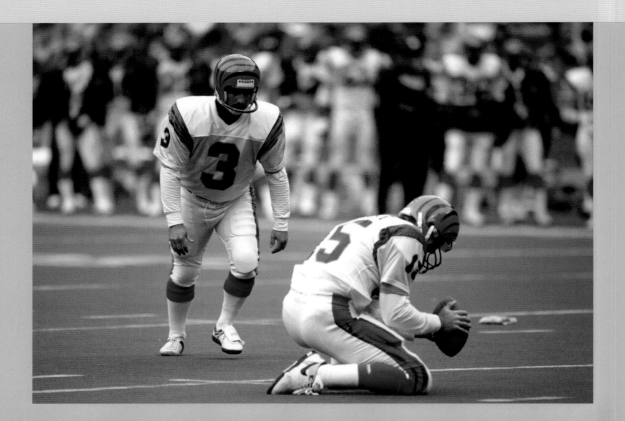

X Over the course of his 13 seasons in Cincinnati, reliable kicker Jim Breech set the Bengals' all-time scoring record with 1,151 points, booting points in 186 straight games.

entertained the fans with the "Ickey Shuffle," a celebratory dance performed in the end zone.

Woods and his teammates danced their way through the playoffs, celebrating first a 21–13 victory over the Seattle Seahawks and then a 21–10 win against the Buffalo Bills in the AFC Championship Game. All that remained was Super Bowl XXIII, held on January 22, 1989, in Miami, where the Bengals would once again meet the San Francisco 49ers. "It's a dream come true," Woods said as the big game approached. "I'm just waiting to score and win the Super Bowl."

But there would be no dancing for Woods and no win for the Bengals in Miami. The offense struggled to move the ball down the field, and the defense suffered a crushing setback

Although injuries cut running back Ickey Woods's career short (he was in the NFL for just four seasons), his touchdown- and dance-filled 1988 season made him a Bengals icon. **X**

BOOMER ESIASON

QUARTERBACK
BENGALS SEASONS: 1984–92, 1997
HEIGHT: 6-FOOT-5
WEIGHT: 224 POUNDS

Norman Julius "Boomer" Esiason's first start as a Bengals player came on a rainy Sunday in October 1984. Although he led Cincinnati to a 13–3 victory over the Houston Oilers that day, the fans didn't get to see any of the gunslinging moves that had defined his college career at the University of Maryland and that would become a hallmark of his professional play. Esiason would go on to toss 247 touchdown passes during his 14-year career, but the only touchdown he scored in that first game was on a quarterback sneak near the muddy goal line. One year later, Esiason took over under center, replacing longtime fan favorite Ken Anderson. Esiason was surprisingly mobile and rushed for almost 1,600 yards during his career. It was his powerful arm, however, that propelled the Bengals to their second Super Bowl appearance, a 20–16 loss to the San Francisco 49ers, in 1988. He left the team five years later to play with the New York Jets and then the Arizona Cardinals, but he returned to Cincinnati to finish his professional playing career with the Bengals in 1997.

when Krumrie's leg was broken during the first quarter. Although the Bengals rebounded in the second half to briefly take the lead, 49ers quarterback Joe Montana broke their hearts by throwing a game-winning touchdown pass with 34 seconds remaining. "It's very disappointing," Esiason said as San Francisco celebrated its 20–16 win. "We were 34 seconds away from a great victory."

Injuries plagued the Bengals the following season. Although Krumrie made an amazing recovery, he wasn't as dominant as he once had been. Woods tore a ligament in his knee in the second game, which sidelined him for the rest of the season, and Esiason struggled with a sore shoulder. McGee posted 1,211 receiving yards, and Brooks galloped for a career-best 1,239 yards, but the 1989 season ended with the Bengals at 8–8 and out of the playoff picture.

Cincinnati's 9–7 record in 1990 earned it a return trip to the playoffs, where the Bengals crushed the Houston Oilers 41–14 in the first round. But the Los Angeles Raiders ended Cincinnati's run a week later, 20–10. Worse yet, team founder and owner Paul Brown died during the off-season. After the deflated Bengals struggled through a 3–13 season in 1991, it was time to rebuild.

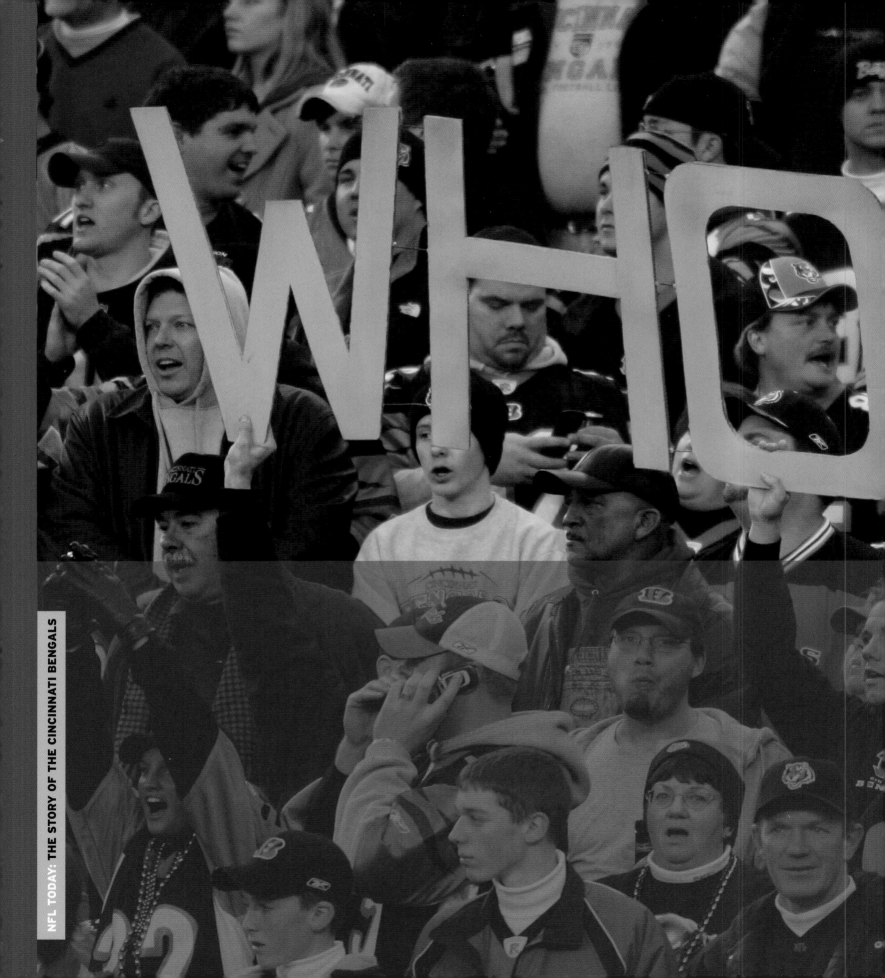

THE WHO DEY STORY

Cincinnati legend has it that the now familiar "Who Dey" chant—which begins with the question, "Who dey think is going to beat them Bengals?" and is followed by "Noooooobooody"—started during the 1981 season. The Bengals were on a roll, and their happy fans were rolling right along with them. The origins of the chant are unclear. Some credit a local beer maker called Hudepohl, whose vendors apparently walked the stadium calling out "Hudey!" instead of "Beer here!"; others say it was stolen from a commercial jingle for a Cincinnati-based auto dealership. However it started, the silly slogan stuck around that whole Super Bowl season and was even recorded as a song by a local television weatherman. By the time the Bengals returned to the Super Bowl in 1988, the chant had gained national recognition. The Who Dey chant is still proudly hollered at Paul Brown Stadium today and is often started by the Bengals' mascot, a smiling tiger in a football jersey whose name just happens to be Who Dey.

FROM BAD
TO WORSE

In 1992, 32-year-old Dave Shula became the youngest head coach in the NFL when he assumed leadership of the Bengals. But he inherited a team made up mostly of aging veterans, and he was committed to injecting new life into the squad. Shula brought in young players such as wide receiver Carl Pickens to accomplish his goal. "I'm hoping to bring a new energy to this franchise," Shula said. "We've got a long way to go, but we're starting today."

Despite the new additions and the contributions of such veterans as running back Harold Green, who rushed for 1,170 yards in 1992, the Bengals fell into the AFC cellar after Muñoz retired in 1992 and Esiason was traded away in 1993. The inexperienced team lost its first 10 games in 1993 and finished the season 3–13—an unfortunate scenario that played itself out again in 1994, when young quarterback Jeff Blake joined the squad.

Cincinnati badly needed a reversal of fortunes. The team hoped that its choice of running back Ki-Jana Carter—a former

X Carl Pickens did his best to boost the struggling Bengals offense in the 1990s, posting an NFL-leading 17 receiving touchdowns in 1995 and making 100 catches in 1996.

ANTHONY MUÑOZ

OFFENSIVE TACKLE
BENGALS SEASONS: 1980-92
HEIGHT: 6-FOOT-6
WEIGHT: 280 POUNDS

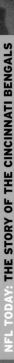

Both local and national sportswriters thought the Bengals were taking a huge risk when they selected offensive tackle Anthony Muñoz with the third overall pick in the 1980 NFL Draft. The mountainous Muñoz had spent much of his final two seasons at the University of Southern California sidelined by knee problems. But the Bengals took a chance on the two-time All-American—and they were roundly rewarded. Muñoz joined the offensive line as a left tackle during his rookie year and was an anchor there for 13 straight seasons. His sheer physical size gave him an advantage in blocking opposing defenders, but his quick feet and sure hands made him a solid receiver as well—he nabbed seven catches and scored four touchdowns during his Hall of Fame career. Muñoz went to the Pro Bowl 11 times and played in 2 Super Bowls, both against the San Francisco 49ers. He retired in 1992 and was inducted into the Pro Football Hall of Fame in 1998. Afterward, Muñoz continued to live near Cincinnati and helped broadcast some of the Bengals' preseason games on a local television station.

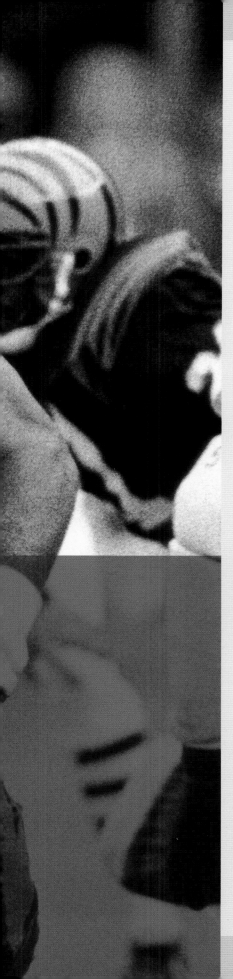

college star from Penn State University—in the 1995 NFL Draft would provide the spark its offense was lacking. But before the regular season even began, Carter blew out a ligament in his knee and missed all of the 1995 season. Still, Blake emerged as a solid starting quarterback: his 3,822 passing yards and 28 touchdowns helped the Bengals improve to 7–9 and earned the young passer a trip to the Pro Bowl.

Despite Blake's efforts and the fancy footwork of running back Garrison Hearst, Coach Shula was fired after the Bengals won just one of their first seven games in 1996. Shula, who

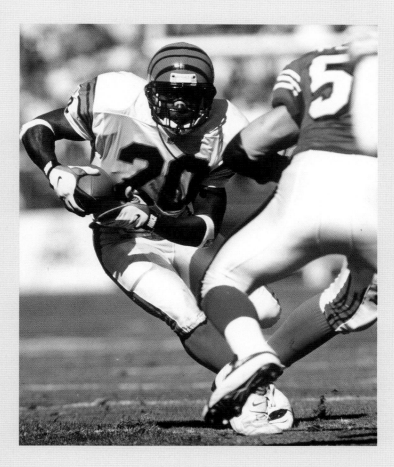

X Typical of the Bengals' bad luck in the '90s, halfback Garrison Hearst became a 49ers star (with 3 straight 1,000-yard seasons) after playing a single season in Cincinnati.

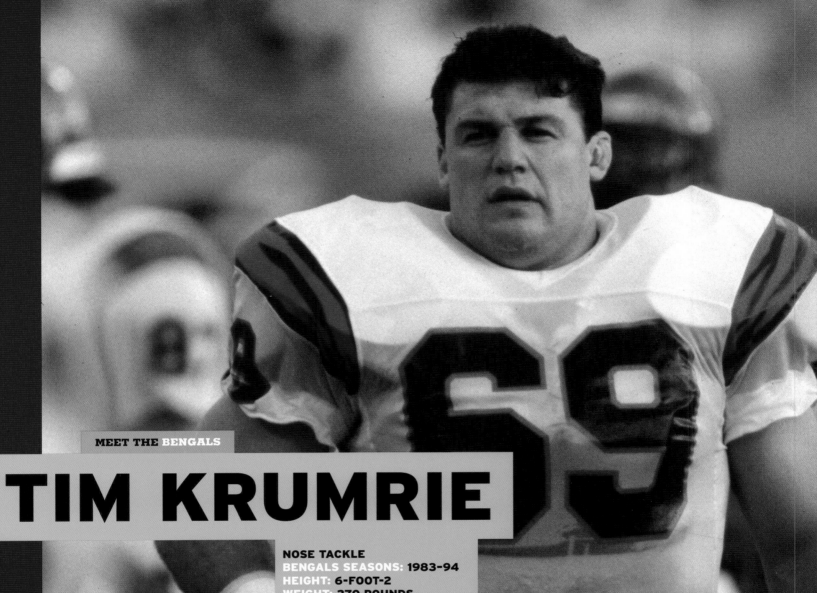

MEET THE BENGALS

TIM KRUMRIE

NOSE TACKLE
BENGALS SEASONS: 1983-94
HEIGHT: 6-FOOT-2
WEIGHT: 270 POUNDS

Tim Krumrie may be best remembered for the sickening sight of his leg being shattered before a television audience of millions as the Bengals battled the San Francisco 49ers in Super Bowl XXIII in January 1989. But Krumrie, who played six more seasons in Cincinnati, is known as one of the best defensive linemen ever to play for the Bengals because of the hits he made—not the hits he took. The Wisconsin native, who grew up on a dairy farm, was known by teammates and opponents alike for his toughness and intensity and quickly established himself as a legend on the defensive line. During his 12-year career with the Bengals, the hulking Krumrie made 1,008 tackles and 34.5 sacks and recovered 13 fumbles. He played in two Pro Bowls; his second appearance, in 1988, was the last time a Bengals defensive lineman has received such recognition. Krumrie retired in 1994, having played his entire career in Cincinnati, and went on to coach for the team as well. By 2008, he was a defensive line coach for the Kansas City Chiefs.

had compiled a disastrous 19–52 record during slightly more than four years with the team, left football entirely to work in his family's chain of steakhouse restaurants. Owner Mike Brown, who had taken over after his father Paul had died, brought back Bruce Coslet, a former Cincinnati tight end and offensive coordinator, to lead the team. The Bengals won seven of their last nine games and finished at an even 8–8.

Coslet wasn't the only familiar face on the Bengals' sidelines in 1997. Former quarterback Ken Anderson had returned as the offensive coordinator, and one-time tackle Tim Krumrie was coaching the defensive line. Even Boomer Esiason came back to finish his career, this time as a backup and mentor to Blake. "There's no hidden agenda or motive on my side," Esiason said. "Jeff is going to let me retire to greener pastures without having to take hits."

But neither Blake nor Esiason, who started the last five games of the season, would be the star of the show in 1997. Instead, it was rookie running back Corey Dillon who shone brightest, amassing 1,129 rushing yards and scoring 10 touchdowns for an otherwise lackluster offense. Dillon was equally impressive in 1998, but again the rest of the offense, led by quarterback Neil O'Donnell, was flat, and the Bengals finished with another losing record.

Nicknamed "Shake 'n Blake" due to his knack for generating big plays, quarterback Jeff Blake was equally adept at scrambling for yardage or heaving long bombs deep down the field. **X**

After watching the Bengals struggle to find the right fit at quarterback, fans had high hopes for the nimble Akili Smith, who had been chosen with the third overall pick in the 1999 NFL Draft. But Smith was benched after struggling as a starter in 1999 and never lived up to the expectations the team had for him. The only bright spots in the disappointing 4–12 season were Dillon's 1,200 rushing yards and kick returner Tremain Mack's club-record average of 27.1 yards per return. As Cincinnati ended the 1990s with a disgraceful 52–108 combined record, the national media began referring to the team as "The Bungles."

SHUFFLING TO THE SUPER BOWL

As the 1988 Bengals marched toward the Super Bowl, an unexpected star shuffled along with them: rookie running back Elbert "Ickey" Woods (pictured), who scored 15 touchdowns in the course of the season. As much as the fans appreciated those points, what they really loved was the dance Woods did in the end zone each time. After each touchdown, he would face the crowds with his arms stretched out wide, then hop twice to the left, twice to the right, spike the ball, and, finally, twirl his right index finger over his head while swiveling his hips and shouting, "Woo! Woo! Woo!" His silly dance was dubbed the "Ickey Shuffle" by the local media, and it was soon being duplicated by teammates, fans, and even team owner Paul Brown, who was 80 years old at the time. Woods's dance sparked Ickey songs, shirts, commercials, and even an Ickey milk shake. More important to Woods, however, was that he was celebrating Cincinnati wins. "I got to do it 15 times that year," he said. "I was in the right place at the right time."

THE
ROAD BACK

X -

Quarterback Jon Kitna excited Cincinnati fans as the new starter in 2001, throwing an NFL-high 581 passes, but the Bengals still posted their 11th straight non-winning season.

On September 10, 2000, more than 64,000 fans gathered for the first game in the state-of-the-art Paul Brown Stadium. After a dismal decade, both the team and its fans were hoping that a new home might reinvigorate the sagging franchise. But when the Bengals fell to the Browns 24–7 that day and were shut out in the next two games as well, it became obvious that Cincinnati needed more than a simple change of scenery to regain its winning ways.

Even though the Bengals finished 4–12, there were signs of improvement during the 2000 season. Slick young receiver Peter Warrick, who scored the first points in Paul Brown Stadium, showed signs of stardom, and Dillon ran his way into the NFL record books with a 278-yard performance in October, breaking Chicago Bears great Walter Payton's record for a single-game rushing total. The Pro Football Hall of Fame honored the hard-charging halfback by displaying the jersey, pants, and cleats he wore that day. "Not many athletes get the opportunity to get their uniform inducted into the Hall of Fame," Dillon said.

But even as individuals were becoming stars, the team as a whole was struggling to come close to achieving a winning season. Veteran Jon Kitna took over for Akili Smith at quarterback in 2001. Helped by a strong, young defense anchored by end Vaughn Booker and linebacker Takeo Spikes, Kitna managed to guide the team to an improved 6–10 record. However, the following year, after recruiting veteran Gus Frerotte as the fifth quarterback to play under center in 5 seasons, the team set a new low, earning just 2 wins and 14 losses.

By the beginning of the 2003 season, new coach Marvin Lewis had reworked the roster so that more than half of the players were new to the team—including Carson Palmer, a strong-armed quarterback taken with the first overall pick in the 2003 NFL Draft. Although Palmer would spend his first season learning from the veteran Kitna, his development was part of Lewis's long-term plan for the Bengals' improvement.

While Palmer watched from the sidelines, Kitna had a sensational 2003 season, connecting with flashy receiver Chad Johnson for 1,355 of his total 3,591 passing yards. After an injury slowed Dillon, Rudi Johnson came off the bench to tally almost 1,000 yards and score 9 touchdowns. Bengals

x As a ballcarrier, Rudi Johnson was both powerful and steady, blasting through opposing defenses to score 12 touchdowns a season in 2004, 2005, and 2006.

BAD BREAKS

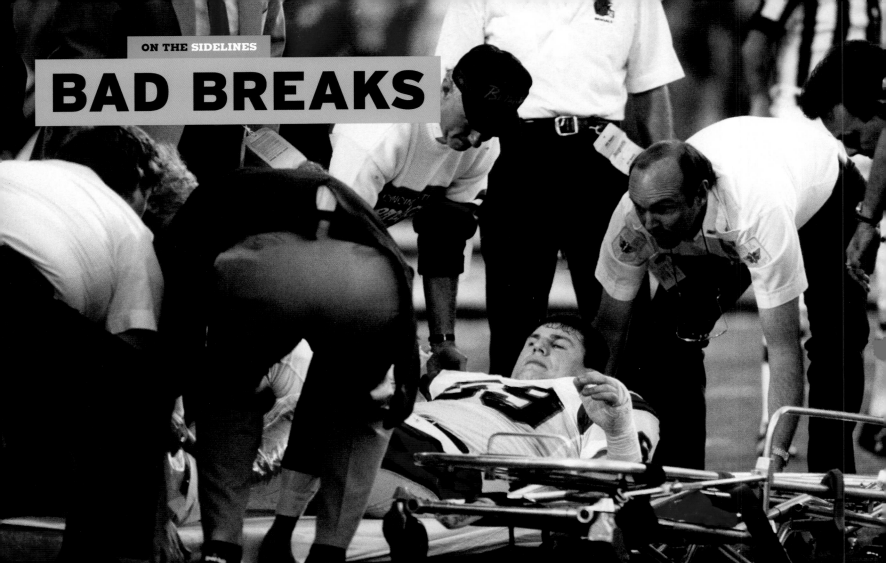

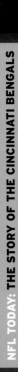

Cincinnati fans have had to share two of their most painful moments with a national audience: first, when nose tackle Tim Krumrie's leg was shattered during Super Bowl XXIII, and then again when quarterback Carson Palmer went down with a shredded knee in the 2005 playoffs. Krumrie's injury was the more gruesome of the two. Television cameras zoomed in to show his leg flopped at an unnatural angle behind him. The cameras remained trained on Krumrie (pictured) as the announcers tried to make sense of what had happened. His tibia, the main bone of the lower leg, was fractured in two places, and his fibula, the outer bone of the lower leg, had snapped as well. A 15-inch steel rod had to be surgically implanted in his leg—but Krumrie showed up at training camp the following season and played six more Bengals seasons. Palmer, whose knee suffered numerous ligament tears, damaged cartilage, and a dislocated kneecap when he was hit by Pittsburgh Steelers defensive tackle Kimo von Oelhoffen, also defied the odds and returned the following season.

X A seventh-round draft pick in 2001, T. J. Houshmandzadeh proved to be a hidden gem, gradually growing into one of football's toughest and most sure-handed wide receivers.

For nearly 30 years, the Cincinnati Bengals shared Riverfront Stadium (which became known as Cinergy Field in 1996) with the Cincinnati Reds baseball team. But in 2000, the Bengals got a brand-new, state-of-the-art stadium of their own: Paul Brown Stadium (pictured), named after the man who had started the team and served as its head coach until 1976. Although the Bengals had sold naming rights for their previous home to Cinergy, an electric utility company, for $6 million, team president Mike Brown wasn't interested in doing the same for the new stadium. He insisted that it bear the name of his father. "We like that our stadium name honors the tradition of the NFL," Brown said. "Many names now don't have anything to do with the game." Cinergy Field, meanwhile, was destroyed. In December 2002, the statuesque old structure came down, imploded section by section with the help of more than 1,200 pounds of dynamite and nitroglycerin. The United Way charity held a raffle to pick one person to push the ceremonial button to bring the building down and raised more than $20,000 in the process.

fans were so charmed by the unassuming young running back that they began cheering "Roo-dee! Roo-dee!" every time he touched the ball. After losing the first three games of the season, the Bengals made a remarkable recovery to finish 8–8 and out of the cellar in the AFC North (which they had joined in 2002). "It was a good year," Coach Lewis said. "Not a great year—a good year."

With Palmer taking over as quarterback, Rudi Johnson running for more than 1,000 yards, and cornerback Tory James snagging 8 interceptions, the Bengals were good again in 2004. Even though the Bengals' 8–8 record left them out of the playoffs, Cincinnati fans celebrated their success all season long with record-setting attendance at Paul Brown Stadium. Each of the eight regular-season home games sold out for the first time since 1992.

Finally, in 2005, those fans were rewarded. The Bengals roared out of the starting blocks with four consecutive wins and ended the season with the division title and an 11–5 record. For the first time in 15 years, the Bengals were in the playoffs, and the city prepared to host the Pittsburgh Steelers in the AFC Wild Card game. Palmer's first pass of the game sailed 66 yards downfield before landing gently in the arms of an open receiver—but back at the line of scrimmage, the

X Young passer Carson Palmer helped make 2005 the Bengals' best season in almost two decades by firing a league-high 32 touchdown passes.

COREY DILLON

RUNNING BACK
BENGALS SEASONS: 1997-2003
HEIGHT: 6-FOOT-1
WEIGHT: 225 POUNDS

Although he had set rushing records as a college standout at the University of Washington, Corey Dillon wasn't immediately snapped up in the 1997 NFL Draft. He was still available in the second round, when the Bengals used the 43rd pick to take the speedy halfback. Dillon immediately made that pick worth the team's while. In his rookie season, he ran for a remarkable 1,129 yards—and that was only the beginning. For each of the next 5 seasons, Dillon surpassed the 1,000-yard mark, including reaching a franchise high of 1,435 yards in 2000. Only once during his 7 seasons with the Bengals did Dillon not reach 1,000 yards, and that was in 2003, when injuries limited him to 541 yards. Although the NFL record he set in Cincinnati for the most yards gained in one game (278 against the Denver Broncos in 2000)—has since been broken, Dillon still holds the team record for most career yards, with 8,061. His fancy footwork is remembered as a bright spot during a dark time for the Bengals—they won 26 games and lost 70 during his tenure.

young quarterback was on the ground, writhing in pain after being hit just as the ball had left his hand. Palmer's knee was badly injured, and his game was over. The Bengals' season also came to an end when the Steelers won, 31–17.

Although some experts had suggested that the injury would end his career, Palmer made an amazing comeback in 2006. T. J. Houshmandzadeh and Chad Johnson both recorded more than 1,000 receiving yards, while cornerback Deltha O'Neal helped spearhead the defense. Unfortunately, the Bengals began to slide downward once again, going 8–8 in 2006 and 7–9 in 2007. Then, as Palmer again struggled with injuries, the 2008 Bengals made an embarrassing plunge to the bottom of the AFC North. Fans were left only with the hope that the return of a healthy Palmer and the improvement of such promising youngsters as cornerback Johnathan Joseph would turn things back around.

The Bengals may have experienced more lows than highs in recent seasons, but the young players in the tiger-striped jerseys take heart in the fact that Cincinnati has been home to some of the NFL's greatest players over the last four decades. Today's Bengals are working to continue that tradition and hope to soon add a Super Bowl jewel to the Queen City's crown.

INDEX